What's a Girl to Do?

WRITTEN BY: **Lillie M. White**

ILLUSTRATIONS BY: **Lesa R. Price**

I dedicate this book to all children suffering with this hardship.

To Bishop Bobbie Hilton and Dr. Valda Hilton, your teachings have quickened my spirit. Thank you.

To Lesa, I could not have done this without you. Your artistic skill and patience brought all my ideas to reality. I am most grateful. Thank you.

To my children and grandchildren, I love you all. May this inspire you to never settle for less than you are.

To my Word family, read and be blessed SPPL.

To order additional copies of this book, contact:
Xlibris
1-888-795-4274
www.Xlibris.com
Orders@Xlibris.com

There are fleas in my carpet.

Bed bugs in my bed . . . and

A millipede in my bath!

I told the fleas they had
to leave.

"All you bed bugs, you must go."

"Mr. Millipede, that bath is for me!

I implored, even said "please".

What did they do?
They laughed at me.

So, I went to Auntie.

I told her why I was blue.
She knew just what to do.

We went to the store, bought a mop,
broom and spray for my room.

Together we cleaned and cleaned. Auntie vacuumed the mattress. I watched as she put a vinyl cover on the mattress.

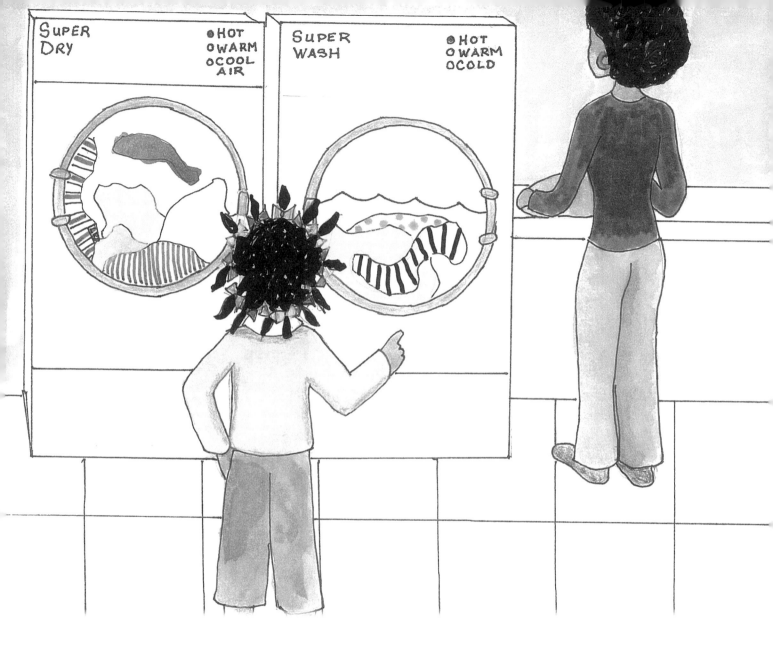

We washed our clothes in hot hot water.

We dusted.
She vacuumed all the floors.

The bed bugs jumped off the bed, ran down the hall, opened the door and shouted, "We're not coming here no more!"

I went to my bath. Mr. Millipede was dressed, clean and sharp as could be. He said, "Excuse me please, I was rude, truly I didn't mean to be. Thank you for the bath, now I must go, exceptional hospitality you have shown."

I sat on my couch, looked around at my beautiful
clean house.

Finally, Auntie and I decided to fix a cup of tea
and have a party.

Keep Bed Bugs Away
Some helpful Tips

1. Clean home daily.

2. Pick one day a week to clean everything in your home.

3. Have your whole family join in, it's fun!

4. Check seats in public places:
Movie Theaters
Schools
Friends houses... etc

5. Put shoes in pillowcase, knot and put in dryer
for 15-20 minutes.

6. Check backpack, purses, and bags before
entering your home.

Steps to Get Rid of Bed Bugs

1. Pick up all clutter and trash on floors.

2. Wash clothes in Hot Hot water.

3. Vacuum bed and mattress

4. Steam mattress and let dry.

5. Put vinyl cover on mattress.

6. Dust.

7. Vacuum all floors.

8. If none of these steps work I advise you to call a professional pest control business. Show this to the adult that cares for you.

The End

שי

מיהולא תבההאו

Printed in the United States
By Bookmasters